Project Title

Another fabulous fanztrivia production

Copyright ©2022 FANZTRIVIA
All rights reserved. This book or any portion thereof may not be reproduced or used in any manner whatsoever without the express permission of the publisher except for the use of brief excerpts in reviews.

CONTENTS

MOTORCYCLE TRIVIA 40 QUESTIONS	5
MOTORCYCLE TRIVIA ANSWERS	26
CLASSIC MOTORCYCLES 40 QUESTIONS	27
CLASSIC MOTORCYCLE ANSWERS	48
MOTORCYCLES IN POP CULTURE 30 QUESTIONS	49
MOTORCYCLE IN POP CULTURE ANSWERS	65
MOTORCYCLE RACING 20 QUESTIONS	66
MOTORCYCLE RACING ANSWERS	77
MOTORCYCLE MYTHS 10 QUESTIONS	78
MOTORCYCLE MYTHS ANSWERS	84
MOTORCYCLE GANGS 10 QUESTIONS	85
MOTORCYCLE GANGS ANSWERS	91
TOTAL SCORE PAGE	92

Project Title

MOTORCYCLE TRIVIA

FORTY QUESTIONS

MOTORCYCLE TRIVIA

Q1 In which country was the first motorcycle invented?

- England — A
- Japan — B
- Germany — C
- France — D

Q2 Most motorcycles have higher MPG rates than cars. True or False?

- True — A
- False — B

MOTORCYCLE TRIVIA

Q 3

What is the approximate ratio of motorcycles to cars worldwide?

- 1 bike for 2 cars — A
- 1 bike for 3 cars — B
- 1 bike for 10 cars — C
- 2 bikes for 1 car — D

Q 4

When was the first internal combustion motorcycle fuelled by petroleum invented?

- 1815 — A
- 1855 — B
- 1885 — C
- 1905 — D

MOTORCYCLE TRIVIA

Q5

In a motorcycle, the rotational force generated by the crankshaft is transmitted to which part?

- Front wheel — A
- Engine — B
- Rear wheel — C
- None of the above — D

Q6

What is the fastest road production motorcycle as of 2022?

- Kawasaki Ninja H2R — A
- Lightning LS-218 — B
- MTT 420-RR — C
- Kawasaki Ninja ZX-14R — D

MOTORCYCLE TRIVIA

Q7

In which city in Italy are Ducatis manufactured?

Rome — A
Bologna — B
Naples — C
Milan — D

Q8

Which company has been the largest motorcycle manufacturer in the world since 1959, with around 400 million models in production by the end of 2019?

Triumph — A
Suzuki — B
Honda — C
Yamaha — D

MOTORCYCLE TRIVIA

Q9 Which of the following models is the first motorcycle to offer an anti-lock braking system?

- Suzuki Cavalcade — A
- Yamaha FJ1200 — B
- Honda Goldwing — C
- BMW K-Series — D

Q10 What was the name of the iconic after market motorcycle helmet visor manufacturer of the 1970s and 80s?

- Tom Heath — A
- Bob Heath — B
- Heath Visors — C
- John Heath — D

MOTORCYCLE TRIVIA

Q11

The motorcycle manufacturer Harley-Davidson is based in which U.S. state?

Missouri — A
Texas — B
Colorado — C
Wisconsin — D

Q12

Who bought the Triumph name and re-established it as one of the world's leading motorcycle manufacturers?

John Bloor — A
Siegfried Bettmann — B
Soichiro Honda — C
William Harley — D

MOTORCYCLE TRIVIA

Q13

What year did Harley Davidson start producing motorcycles?

1903 | A
1893 | B
1913 | C
1923 | D

Q14

What is the world record speed for the fastest motorcycle wheelie?

179.2mph | A
191.3mph | B
199.7mph | C
185.3mph | D

MOTORCYCLE TRIVIA

Q15 There are three main ways to classify motorcycle engines: the number of strokes in the power cycles, the capacity of the combustion chambers, and the number of what?

Gears — A
Axlesl — B
Cylinders — C
Exhaust pipes — D

Q16 What nationality was the original founder of Triumph motorcycles?

Hungarian — A
German — B
English — C
Welsh — D

MOTORCYCLE TRIVIA

Q17

Complete the famous slogan of the Indian motorcycle brand Royal Enfield: "Built like a …"

Gun — A
Tank — B
Car — C
Bullet — D

Q18

Which part of a motorcycle consists of the brakes, wheels, suspension, and frame?

Chassis — A
Body — B
Channel — C
Fairing — D

MOTORCYCLE TRIVIA

Q19

Which car manufacturer is the owner of the motorcycle brand Ducati?

Ferrari A

BMW B

Volkswagen C

Fiat D

Q20

Which Canadian electric motorcycle is designed with adjustable ergonomics?

Ecobike A

Ego B

DSR C

Hypersport D

MOTORCYCLE TRIVIA

Q21 Which motorcycle brand has crossed tuning forks as its logo?

Suzuki — A
Honda — B
Yamaha — C
Royal Enfield — D

Q22 What somewhat unflattering nickname is given to a motorcycle that is built for speed and not for comfort?

Bottom Basher — A
Crotch Rocket — B
Pocket Rocket — C
Knee Scraper — D

MOTORCYCLE TRIVIA

Q23 How far was the longest backwards motorcycle ride achieved by an Indian rider in 2014?

- Around 3km — A
- Around 10km — B
- Around 500km — C
- Around 200km — D

Q24 A motorcycle with long forks and an overall stretched-out appearance is called what?

- Scrambler — A
- Cafe Racer — B
- Chopper — C
- Street bike — D

MOTORCYCLE TRIVIA

Q25

What are "ape hangers"?

- Very loud motorcycles — A
- Very low handlebars — B
- Very tall handlebars — C
- Very tall riders — D

Q26

Along with Japan, which country mainly dominates the world's motorcycle industry in the 21st century?

- Brazil — A
- China — B
- India — C
- Germany — D

MOTORCYCLE TRIVIA

Q27

By the time World War I broke out, which country was the world's largest motorcycle manufacturer?

United Kingdom | A
India | B
United States | C
Japan | D

Q28

Which motorcycle model by Honda became the world's biggest selling vehicle of all time with more than 60 million units manufactured in 2008?

Grom | A
Ruckus | B
Super Cub | C
Goldwing | D

MOTORCYCLE TRIVIA

Q29

In 1884, an inventor from which country coined the term motorcycle after he invented a 3-wheeled petrol vehicle?

France A
Italy B
United states C
Great Britain D

Q30

What is a Spyder?

A motorcycle with 3 seats A
A motorcycle with 3 wheels B
A motorcycle with 3 gears C
A motorcycle with 3 lights D

MOTORCYCLE TRIVIA

Q31 The world's smallest motorcycle was made by Tom Wiberg in 2003 in Sweden. What is it called?

- Tinybike — A
- Smallbike — B
- Minibke — C
- Smalltoe — D

Q32 What is the world record for the longest distance that a man can ride a motorcycle in one day?

- More than 3000km — A
- More than 5000km — B
- More than 500km — C
- More than 6000km — D

MOTORCYCLE TRIVIA

Q33

If a motorcyclist says he has "road rash," what does this tell you?

A. She/he has had an accident
B. She/he is ill
C. She/he is addicted to motorcycling
D. She/he has a rusty motorcycle

Q34

Two of the three founders of Harley-Davidson were brothers. True or False?

A. False
B. True

MOTORCYCLE TRIVIA

Q35 Suzuki, one of the most popular motorcycle manufacturers from Japan, started its business in which industry?

- Oil and gas — A
- Mining — B
- Looming — C
- Fishing — D

Q36 When a motorcycle is said to be a "naked bike," what does that mean?

- Without engine — A
- Standard, no frills — B
- Unpainted — C
- Not built yet — D

MOTORCYCLE TRIVIA

Q37

What is a 'stoppie'?

- Reverse wheelie — A
- Speeding ticket — B
- Flat tyre — C
- Broken down — D

Q38

The 'motorcycle salute' is made with two fingers. True or False?

- True — A
- False — B

MOTORCYCLE TRIVIA

Q39 What part, which is no longer used much in cars, is still in use today on many motorcycles?

- brakes — A
- alternator — B
- carburettor — C
- timing belt — D

Q40 When it comes to the clothing you wear on a motorcycle, which is the correct phrase?

- Dress for the ease, not the breeze. — A
- Dress for the ride, not the slide. — B
- Dress for the wind, not the bend. — C
- Dress for the slide, not the ride. — D

MOTORCYCLE TRIVIA

YOUR SCORE:

/40

ANSWERS:

1 C
2 A
3 D
4 C
5 C
6 C
7 B
8 C
9 D
10 B
11 D
12 A
13 A
14 B
15 C
16 B
17 A
18 A
19 C
20 D
21 C
22 B
23 D
24 C
25 C
26 C
27 B
28 C
29 D
30 B
31 D
32 A
33 A
34 B
35 C
36 B
37 A
38 A
39 C
40 D

CLASSIC MOTORCYCLES

FORTY QUESTIONS

CLASSIC MOTORCYCLES

Q1

Honda's first true motorcycle was built in 1950. What was it called?

Dream — A
Helix — B
Monkey — C
Goldwing — D

Q2

How many US motorcycle manufacturers were there at the start of the 20th century?

Thousands — A
Hundreds — B
Ten — C
Two — D

CLASSIC MOTORCYCLES

Q3 Vintage bikes are generally considered those made before which year?

- No set year | A
- 1974 | B
- 1982 | C
- 1963 | D

Q4 Who did T. E. Lawrence name his motorcycles after?

- British actors | A
- US Presidents | B
- British Kings | C
- Girlfriends | D

CLASSIC MOTORCYCLES

Q5 In what year did Moto Guzzi celebrate it's hundredth anniversary?

2001 A
2021 B
1991 C
1981 D

Q6 At the time of their release, some Brough Superior motorcycles cost as much as what?

A holiday A
A car B
A house C
A bicycle D

CLASSIC MOTORCYCLES

Q7 What famous manufacturer was responsible for the Gloria model sidecar?

- Honda — A
- Ariel — B
- BSA — C
- Triumph — D

Q8 Fred Watson founded which company in 1912?

- Sidecar Ltd — A
- Watsonian Squire — B
- Fred's Sidecars — C
- Watson Wagons — D

CLASSIC MOTORCYCLES

Q9 What was Yamaha making when it first opened in 1887?

Cars A
Tyres B
Pianos C
Bicycles D

Q10 What was Triumph making when it first opened in 1888?

Bicycles A
Pianos B
Tyres C
Cars D

CLASSIC MOTORCYCLES

Q11 Which motorcycle manufacturer was the world's largest by 1964?

Honda — A
Triumph — B
Yamaha — C
BSA — D

Q12 What was Suzuki making when it first opened?

Printing presses — A
Trams — B
Pianos — C
Weaving looms — D

CLASSIC MOTORCYCLES

Q13

Which motorcycle manufacturer was the first to patent and use telescopic forks in 1932?

BMW — A
Yamaha — B
Honda — C
Ariel — D

Q14

What did Indian make when it first opened in the 19th century?

Bicycles — A
Weaving looms — B
Watches — C
Guitars — D

CLASSIC MOTORCYCLES

Q15 What year did the Triumph Bonneville launch?

1963 A
1950 B
1959 C
1958 D

Q16 Which of the following is considered to be the world's rarest motorcycle?

Trubet A
Traub B
Trenten C
Trazin D

CLASSIC MOTORCYCLES

Q17 Which one of the following 1930s motorcycles had a top speed of 110mph?

- A. Vincent Rapide
- B. Brough Superior Austin Four
- C. Crocker V-Twin
- D. Ariel Square Four

Q18 How much did the 1978 Honda CBX1000 weigh?

- A. 432kg
- B. 272kg
- C. 198kg
- D. 174kg

CLASSIC MOTORCYCLES

Q219 What year was the Royal Enfield Continental GT launched?

- 1961 A
- 1970 B
- 1959 C
- 1965 D

Q220 Which 1970s motorcycle became known as 'The Widowmaker'?

- Kawasaki Mach III H1 A
- Triumph Bonneville B
- Harley Davidson XR750 C
- BMW R90S D

CLASSIC MOTORCYCLES

Q21 What was the top speed of the Vincent Black Shadow?

125mph A
115mph B
135mph C
118mph D

Q22 What year was the Norton Commando launched?

1959 A
1967 B
1969 C
1960 D

CLASSIC MOTORCYCLES

223 What addition to motorcycles most improved their top speed in the 1980s?

- Fairings — A
- Fuel mixtures — B
- Weight reduction — C
- Larger engines — D

224 In the 1920s, what did a motorcyle model number usually indicate?

- Total number produced — A
- Cylinder size — B
- Top speed in mph — C
- Size of petrol tank — D

CLASSIC MOTORCYCLES

Q25 The "Ace" was a model of motorcycle made by which car and bike manufacturer?

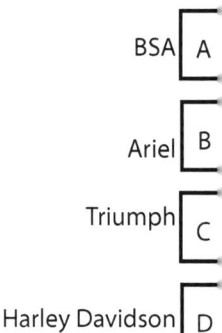

BSA A
Ariel B
Triumph C
Harley Davidson D

Q26 What year was the Honda CB750 launched?

1949 A
1959 B
1969 C
1979 D

CLASSIC MOTORCYCLES

Q27 What year did Triumph end production?

1987 A
1984 B
1991 C
1988 D

Q28 The Yamaha DT-1 was the first mass produced type of what motorcycle?

Chopper A
Enduro B
Off road C
Cafe Racer D

CLASSIC MOTORCYCLES

Q29

What year was the Kawasaki Z1 launched?

1952 A
1962 B
1972 C
1982 D

Q30

What year was the last Vincent motorcycle produced?

1955 A
1965 B
1975 C
1985 D

CLASSIC MOTORCYCLES

Q31 For how many years in a row from 1947 did Nortons win the Isle of Man TT?

- A: 8 years
- B: 6 years
- C: 10 years
- D: 4 years

Q32 What were the owners of new BSA Gold Stars given when they collected their motorcycle from the factory?

- A: A standing ovation
- B: A spare wheel
- C: A custom helmet
- D: Dynamometer test results

CLASSIC MOTORCYCLES

Q33 Who helped design the famous Norton logo?

- James Norton's daughter | A
- James's Norton's son | B
- James Norton's wife | C
- James's Norton's sister? | D

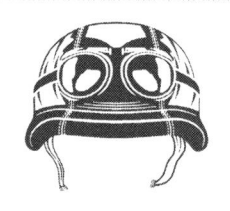

Q34 Which of the following was not a Vincent motorcycle model?

- Meteor | A
- Comet | B
- Asteroid | C
- Rapide | D

CLASSIC MOTORCYCLES

Q35 The Black Shadow and Black Prince were manufactured by which brand?

Ariel — A
Triumph — B
Vincent Motorcycles — C
BSA — D

Q36 How many Norton Commandos were produced between 1967 and 1977?

120,000 — A
60,000 — B
25,000 — C
1.2 million — D

CLASSIC MOTORCYCLES

Q37 What do the letters BSA stand for?

- British Safety Arms — A
- Basingstoke Short Arms — B
- Birmingham Small Arms — C
- Bristol Single Ace — D

Q38 Which motorcycle do many enthusiasts consider to be the first 'modern' super bike?

- BSA Rocket Gold Star — A
- Honda CB750 — B
- Norton Commando — C
- Harley Davidson Electraglide — D

CLASSIC MOTORCYCLES

Q39 Which 1980s motorcycle had a top speed of 169mph?

- Yamaha FJ1200 — A
- Kawasaki ZX-10 — B
- Suzuki GSX-R1100 — C
- Yamaha FZR1000 EXUP — D

Q40 What make of motorcycle was Lawrence of Arabia riding when he was killed in Dorset in 1936?

- Brough Superior — A
- BSA Gold Stari — B
- Ariel Square Four — C
- Vincent Comet — D

CLASSIC MOTORCYCLES

YOUR SCORE:

/40

ANSWERS:

1 A
2 B
3 A
4 C
5 B
6 C
7 D
8 C
9 C
10 A
11 A
12 D
13 A
14 C
15 C
16 B
17 C
18 B
19 D
20 A
21 A
22 B
23 A
24 C
25 B
26 C
27 D
28 C
29 C
30 A
31 A
32 D
33 A
34 C
35 C
36 B
37 C
38 B
39 D
40 A

MOTORCYCLES IN POPULAR CULTURE

THIRTY QUESTIONS

MOTORCYCLES IN POPULAR CULTURE

Q1 Billy Joel's 1980 hit 'You May Be Right' included a line about about riding his motorcycle in the rain.
True or False?

True A
False B

Q2 The motorcycle that Arnold Schwarzenegger rides through Los Angeles's canals in "Terminator 2: Judgment Day" is a BMW.
True or False?

False A
True B

MOTORCYCLES IN POPULAR CULTURE

Q3 Which famous actor rode a motorcycle over a German prison camp's fence in 1963's "The Great Escape"?

- James Dean — A
- Charlie Chaplin — B
- Marlon Brando — C
- Steve McQueen — D

Q4 Who starred in the 1935 film "No Limit", about the Isle of Man TT?

- Burt Reynolds — A
- Clark Gable — B
- Gary Cooper — C
- George Formby — D

MOTORCYCLES IN POPULAR CULTURE

Q5 What is the name of the motorcycle gang in the 1953 film The Wild One starring Marlon Brando?

- A. The Lost Boys
- B. The White Riders
- C. The Hells Bells
- D. The Black Rebels

Q6 Which Rolling Stone Magazine writer rode with the Hell's Angels for a year in order to write a tell-all book?

- A. Truman Capote
- B. Lester Bangs
- C. Cameron Crowe
- D. Hunter S. Thompson

MOTORCYCLES IN POPULAR CULTURE

Q 7

Which of the following celebrities has founded his own brand of motorcycle?

- Kanye West — A
- Keanu Reeves — B
- Tom Cruise — C
- Eminem — D

Q 8

What motorcycle did Prince ride in his Purple Rain video?

- Kawasaki Ninja GPZ900R — A
- Honda Shadow 750 — B
- Hondamatic CM400a — C
- Ducati Paso 750 — D

MOTORCYCLES IN POPULAR CULTURE

Q9 Which motorcycle did Arnold Schwarzenegger ride in Terminator 2?

- A. BMW R1200C
- B. Yamaha Virago 535
- C. Harley Davidson Fat Boy
- D. Suzuki Intruder

Q10 In which of the following famous movies did Marlon Brando star as the leader of a menacing bike gang?

- A. A Streetcar Named Desire
- B. On the Waterfront
- C. The Wild One
- D. Last Tango in Paris

MOTORCYCLES IN POPULAR CULTURE

Q11 Which 1970s TV series in the US is thought to have made motorcycles family friendly?

- Wonder Woman — A
- CHiPs — B
- MASH — C
- The Waltons — D

Q12 Who originally sang "Born to Be Wild," the famous rock song that starts with the sound of a revving motorcycle?

- U2 — A
- Elvis — B
- Steppenwolf — C
- Queen — D

MOTORCYCLES IN POPULAR CULTURE

Q13 Which band originally sang the song containing the lyrics "It's not a big motorcycle, just a groovy little motorbike"?

- A. The Beatles
- B. The Rolling Stones
- C. The Doors
- D. The Beach Boys

Q14 Which of these actors did NOT star as a biker in the 1969 classic road film, "Easy Rider"?

- A. Jack Nicholson
- B. Dennis Hopper
- C. Robert De Niro
- D. Henry Fonda

MOTORCYCLES IN POPULAR CULTURE

Q15 What was written on the poster advertising 1969 biker movie 'Run Angel, Run'?

- A. raw and violent
- B. peace and love
- C. live free
- D. rebel riders

Q16 What's the name of the motorcycle Batman uses to fight the Joker in "The Dark Knight"?

- A. Batbike
- B. Batpod
- C. Batwheels
- D. Batoutahell

MOTORCYCLES IN POPULAR CULTURE

Q17 Which make of motorcycle did the stars of CHiPs ride?

Kawasaki A
Harley Davidson B
Triumph C
Honda D

Q18 What historical figure's life story is told in the movie, "The Motorcycle Diaries"?

Che Guevara A
Lenin B
Barak Obama C
Donald trump D

MOTORCYCLES IN POPULAR CULTURE

Q19 **What bike did Marlon Brando ride in 'The Wild Ones'?**

Triumph Thunderbird — A
Norton Commando — B
Brough Superior — C
Harley Davidson — D

Q20 **Complete the title of the Anthony Hopkins motorcycle movie from 2005: "The World's Fastest _____".**

American — A
Man — B
Indian — C
Motorcycle — D

MOTORCYCLES IN POPULAR CULTURE

Q21 **What motorbike does Trinity ride in 'The Matrix'?**

- A. Triumph Speed Triple
- B. Ducati Monster 1100S
- C. KTM Super Duke
- D. Suzuki Bandit

Q22 **Which band had a motorcyle related hit with 'Leader of the Pack' in the 1960s?**

- A. The Beach Boys
- B. The Beatles
- C. Shangri Las
- D. Steppenwolf

MOTORCYCLES IN POPULAR CULTURE

Q23 What motorcycle does Trinity ride in 'The Matrix Reloaded'?

- A. Triumph Daytona 955i
- B. Honda CBR900 RR
- C. Ducati 996
- D. Harley Davidson Fat Boy

Q24 What is the motorcyle on Meatloaf's Bat Out of Hell album cover powered by?

- A. Nuclear power
- B. Petrol engine
- C. Electric motor
- D. Jet engine

MOTORCYCLES IN POPULAR CULTURE

Q25 Gastronomers Si & Dave are better known as who?

- A. The Bearded Bikers
- B. Motor Cookers
- C. The Bike Chefs
- D. The Hairy Bikers

Q26 What was Judge Dredd's motorcycle called?

- A. Lawmaster
- B. Masterful
- C. Dredd Bike
- D. Hellcycle

MOTORCYCLES IN POPULAR CULTURE

Q27 Which one of the following stars did not ride Triumph motorcycles?

- Charlie Chaplin — A
- James Dean — B
- Bob Dylan — C
- Steve McQueen — D

Q28 What make of motorcycle is used to jump the fence in 'The Great Escape'?

- BMW — A
- Harley Davidson — B
- Triumph — C
- Jawa — D

MOTORCYCLES IN POPULAR CULTURE

Q29

How much did Tom Cruise pay for his Vyrus 987 C3 NV?

A. $78,000
B. $1.3 million it
C. $104,000
D. $230,000

Q30

What motorcycle does Uma Thurman ride in 'Kill Bill'?

A. Suzuki GPX250
B. Kawasaki 250 Ninja
C. Kawasaki ZZR250
D. Honda CB250

MOTORCYCLES IN POPULAR CULTURE

YOUR SCORE:

/30

ANSWERS:

1 A
2 A
3 D
4 D
5 D
6 A
7 B
8 C
9 C
10 C
11 B
12 C
13 D
14 C
15 A
16 B
17 A
18 A
19 A
20 C
21 A
22 C
23 C
24 D
25 D
26 A
27 A
28 C
29 C
30 C

MOTORCYCLE RACING

TWENTY QUESTIONS

MOTORCYCLE RACING

Q1

What's the final bend at Brands Hatch called?

Widowmaker A
Clarke Curve B
Hairpin C
Park Curve D

Q2

In which American state is Pikes Peak?

Ohio A
Texas B
California C
Colorado D

MOTORCYCLE RACING

Q3 How many British Superbike titles did Ryucihi Kiyonari win?

- None A
- Three B
- Two C
- Four D

Q4 Who was contracted to receive $10 million for the 2017 MotoGP season?

- Jorge Lorenzo A
- Valentino Rossi B
- Marc Marquez C
- Eugene Laverty D

MOTORCYCLE RACING

Q 5

Who was the first female rider to race solo in the Isle of Man TT?

Jenny Tinmouth	A
Maria Costello	B
Hayley Jayne Capewell	C
Beryl Swain	D

Q 6

Where is the Australian MotoGP held?

Paul Island	A
Phillip Island	B
Peter Island	C
Patrick Island	D

MOTORCYCLE RACING

Q7 How many back-to-back MotoGP titles did Michael Doohan win?

- Seven — A
- Five — B
- Three — C
- Four — D

Q8 What year did Casey Stoner retire from motorcycle racing?

- 2011 — A
- 2014 — B
- 2012 — C
- 2010 — D

MOTORCYCLE RACING

Q9 At which Grand Prix did Wayne Rainey have the crash that ended his career?

- Spanish — A
- British — B
- Brazilian — C
- Italian — D

Q10 As of 2022, who is the most successful Spanish motorcyle racer of all time?

- Àlex Crivillé — A
- Marc Márquez — B
- Dani Pedrosa — C
- Jorge Lorenzo — D

MOTORCYCLE RACING

Q11 How many Grand Prix World Championships has Valentino Rossi won?

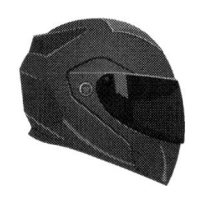

- A. Six
- B. Twelve
- C. Three
- D. Nine

Q12 As of 2022, who is considered to be the greatest motorcycle racer of all time?

- A. Michael Doohan
- B. Jorge Lorenzo
- C. Valentino Rossi
- D. Giacomo Agostini

MOTORCYCLE RACING

Q13 Who pioneered the cornering method of extended knees?

- John Surtees — A
- Valentino Rossi — B
- Kenny Roberts — C
- Mike Hailwood — D

Q14 Mike Hailwood's nickname was "Mike the _____"

- Trike — A
- Spike — B
- Strike — C
- Bike — D

MOTORCYCLE RACING

Q15 As of 2022, who holds the female lap record of the Isle of Man TT?

- A. Jenny Tinmouth
- B. Maria Costello
- C. Hayley Jayne Capewell
- D. Beryl Swain

Q16 Who is the only person to have won world titles on both two and four wheels?

- A. Kenny Roberts
- B. John Surtees
- C. Valentino Rossi
- D. Mike hailwood

MOTORCYCLE RACING

Q17 What year did the Paris-Dakar Rally start?

1979 A
1959 B
1969 C
1989 D

Q18 How long does each Motocross World Championship race last?

45 minutes A
15 minutes B
1 hour C
30 minutes D

MOTORCYCLE RACING

Q19 As of 2022, who holds the outright lap record of the Isle of Man TT?

A. Michael Rutter
B. Dean Harrison
C. Peter Hickman
D. Michael Dunlop

Q20 How many gears does a speedway bike have?

A. Three
B. Two
C. Four
D. One

MOTORCYCLE RACING

YOUR SCORE: /20

ANSWERS:
1 B
2 D
3 B
4 C
5 D
6 B
7 B
8 C
9 D
10 D
11 D
12 D
13 C
14 D
15 A
16 B
17 A
18 D
19 C
20 D

MOTORCYCLE MYTHS

TEN QUESTIONS

MOTORCYCLE MYTHS

Q1 What colour is considered unlucky for a motorcycle racer?

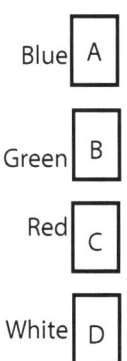

Blue — A
Green — B
Red — C
White — D

Q2 Some bikers believe it's bad luck to ride solo with the rear pegs down. True or False?

True — A
False — B

MOTORCYCLE MYTHS

Q 3

Small objects on the road always cause motorcycle crashes.

True or False?

True A
False B

Q 4

Loud motorcycle exhaust pipes save lives.

True or False?

True A
False B

MOTORCYCLE MYTHS

Q 5

'As a motorcycle rider, I'm too good/cautious/young/old to crash.'

True or False?

True ☐ A

False ☐ B

Q 6

Cars cause most motorcycle accidents.

True or False?

True ☐ A

False ☐ B

MOTORCYCLE MYTHS

Q7

Don't use your front brake unless you have to.

True or False?

True A
False B

Q8

ABS braking isn't safe.

True or False?

True A
False B

MOTORCYCLE MYTHS

Q9

Helmets increase the likliehood of spinal injuries.
True or False?

True A

False B

Q10

Full face helmets block your field of view.
True or False?

True A

False B

MOTORCYCLE MYTHS

YOUR SCORE: /10

ANSWERS:
1 A
2 A
3 B
4 B
5 B
6 B
7 B
8 B
9 B
10 B

MOTORCYCLE GANGS

TEN QUESTIONS

MOTORCYCLE GANGS

Q1

Which was the original US outlaw motorcycle gang?

The Bandidos — A
The Pagans — B
The Hell's Angels — C
The Outlaws — D

Q2

Which is the world's largest outlaw motorcycle gang?

The Pagans — A
The Outlaws — B
The bandidos — C
The Hell's Angels — D

MOTORCYCLE GANGS

Q3 All motorcycle clubs are considered outlaw groups. True or False?

True A

False B

Q4 According to the US Bureau of Alcohol, Tobacco and Firearms, the Mongols Motorcycle Club is the "most violent and dangerous" in the United States. True or False?

True A

False B

MOTORCYCLE GANGS

Q5 Motorcycle gang members wear different colored wings on their jackets representing deviant sex acts they've engaged in. True or False?

True A
False B

Q6 One of the most common criminal enterprises among outlaw motorcycle gangs is involvement in the illicit drug trade. True or False?

True A
False B

MOTORCYCLE GANGS

Q7 Members who leave outlaw motorcycle clubs must have any tattoos with the clubs' logos removed.

True or False?

True A

False B

Q8 Larger gangs, like the Mongols and Hells Angels, have copyrighted the images of their club colors.
True or False?

True A

False B

MOTORCYCLE GANGS

Q9

Unlike street gangs, motorcycle gangs don't use their "colors" to claim their turf.

True or False?

True A
False B

Q10

Outlaw motorcycle gangs are uniquely American; none have been formed in any other countries.

True or False?

True A
False B

MOTORCYCLE GANGS

YOUR SCORE: /10

ANSWERS:
1 D
2 D
3 B
4 A
5 B
6 A
7 A
8 A
9 B
10 B

YOUR SCORES:

MOTORCYCLE TRIVIA:	/40
CLASSIC MOTORCYCLES:	/40
MOTORCYCLES IN POPULAR CULTURE:	/30
MOTORCYCLE RACING	/20
MOTORCYCLE MYTHS:	/10
MOTORCYCLE GANGS	/10

TOTAL SCORE /150

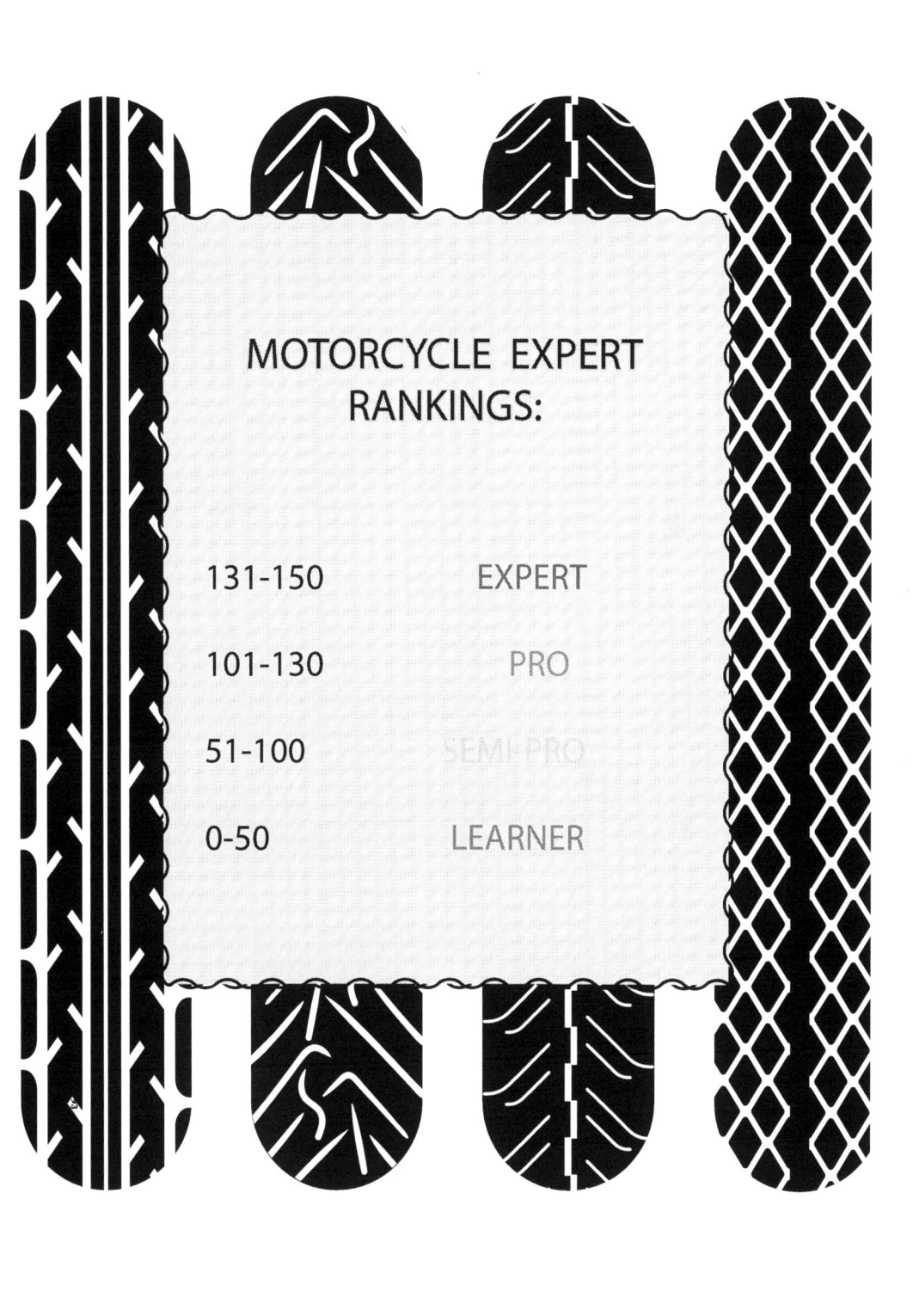

MOTORCYCLE EXPERT RANKINGS:

131-150	EXPERT
101-130	PRO
51-100	SEMI-PRO
0-50	LEARNER

IF YOU'VE ENJOYED
THIS QUIZ AS MUCH
AS WE HAVE...

WE'D LOVE IT
IF YOU'D LEAVE US...

A FAB 5 STAR REVIEW!!

MANY THANKS FROM
THE FANZMEDIA
TEAM!!!!

Printed in Great Britain
by Amazon